Ferry Farm Focus
96-97

EARLY LEARNING EXPERIENCES IN CRITICAL THINKING

by Imogene Forte and Joy MacKenzie

Incentive Publications, Inc.
Nashville, Tennessee

Illustrated by Gayle Seaberg Harvey
Edited by Jan Keeling

ISBN 0-86530-325-8

PRINTED IN THE UNITED STATES OF AMERICA

Table Of Contents

About This Book . . .

Early Learning Experiences in Critical Thinking has been planned to help young children learn through experimentation, through creative involvement in directed activities, and finally, through the joy of discovery.

Young children are curious about and extremely sensitive to their environment. They instinctively push and pull, take apart and attempt to put together again, smell, taste, feel, and listen to things around them. "Why?" "What?" "When?" "Where?" and "How?" are words they use naturally and often. It is this interaction with their environment that parents and teachers can either nurture and encourage or inhibit and retard. Children who have had many happy, satisfying opportunities to use their hands, feet, eyes, ears, and whole bodies are much more apt to adjust happily and successfully to more structured learning experiences.

The purpose of the activities in *Early Learning Experiences in Critical Thinking* is to help children understand and appreciate their environment, to develop self-awareness, to express themselves creatively, and to provide enjoyment and appreciation of literature.

The book includes a mix of simple hands-on activities, free-choice activities, and more structured teacher-directed activities. While instructions are directed to the child, an adult will, of course, need to read and interact with the child in the interpretation and completion of the activities. Ideally, the projects will be presented in a stress-free setting that will afford time for the child to question, explore, wonder, ponder, and create—and to develop an abiding, imaginatively inquisitive approach to creative self-expression. The fanciful illustrations will provide added incentive for lively interaction. Each activity is intended to contribute to the development of skills and concepts which will enhance the child's self-concept and serve as a guide to personal achievement.

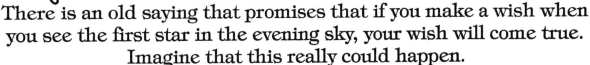

Wish upon a Star

There is an old saying that promises that if you make a wish when you see the first star in the evening sky, your wish will come true. Imagine that this really could happen.
Choose a friend for whom you would like to make three special wishes. Write your friend's name on the line below.
Then write each of your special wishes on one of the stars below.

I wish my friend _____ could have these three wishes.

How do you think your friend would respond if the wishes came true? Would he or she have chosen the same wishes or might he or she have made different wishes?

My Name Is _____

Think Ahead

Something is terribly wrong here. What is it? Can you fix it?

Trace or cut out the heads on this page and see if you can
place each one properly on the next page.
Attach the heads with tape or glue. Then color your picture.

My Name Is _____

11

Do You Know Your ABCs?

Each letter of the alphabet in the list below sounds like a word that could be the answer to a clue in the other list. Draw a line from each letter to the clue it matches.

Clues	Letters
A vegetable	B
The ocean	T
A question	C
A drink	J
A girl's name	E
An insect	U
A scream	P
A body part	Y
A boy's name	K
A female sheep	I

My Name Is _____

Lifesavers

Pretend that you are on an ocean fishing trip. Somehow you have become lost and cannot find your way to shore. It is getting dark, and you do not know when you may be rescued.

If you could choose only one other person and only five possessions to have with you, who and what would you choose? Think carefully about what you would need to survive and what kind of person would be most helpful to you.
Write the names of your choices in the lifesavers below. Be ready to tell why you chose each one.

My Name Is _____

Body Talk

Have you noticed that a person's body
often shows how she or he is feeling?
You can tell a lot about a person by the way he walks
or by the expression she has on her face.

Draw a line from each word to a picture that shows
how you might look as you entered a room feeling . . .

angry   disappointed

sad   lonely

excited   very important

hurt   embarrassed

My Name Is _____

Unbutton Your Skin!

Suppose you are getting out of the bath one day, and you look down to discover that your bare skin has buttons on it. You slowly and carefully unbutton the top button and look inside. It looks strange. It's not really you inside!

What would you do? Would you
  1) keep unbuttoning to find out what would happen?
                    OR
  2) button back up and hope the buttons would soon disappear?

What if you found you were a panda bear or a robot or a space creature underneath? Would you take a chance and step out of your skin?

Would you take off your skin if you knew you could always put it back on whenever you wished?

Would you take it off if you knew you could NEVER put it on again?

Tell how you think you would act and tell why you would act that way.

All to Pieces

This poor creature has gone all to pieces.
Cut around the frame of his picture.
Then cut on the solid lines to separate the pieces.
See if you can put him back together the way he's supposed to be.
Paste each piece perfectly in place.
If he is smiling, then you must have done a good job. Color him happy!

CUT

16

The Perfect Fit

Look at the shape of each container.
Which would be a good home or hiding place for a turtle?
For blueberry syrup?
For uncooked spaghetti?
For a pet worm?
For tiger toenails?
For jelly beans?

Think of an object you might keep or store that would fit just fine
in each container.

17

Stop, Look, and Listen

I have two , the better to see with.

I have two , the better to hear with.

As I've used my , I've learned that some things I see make me sad, and some make me glad.

As I've used my , I've learned that some things I hear make me cry, and some make me laugh.

Here is something that I see that makes me sad.

Here is something that I see that makes me glad.

This is something that I hear that makes me cry.

This is something that I hear that makes me laugh.

My Name Is _____

What's on Your Mind?

What kinds of things do you think about most often?
What do you worry about?
What do you dream about?

Draw a pretend picture of your brain on the next page.
Can you show which kinds of thoughts take up the
most space in your brain?

Read the list below.
Find a crayon of the right color to represent each subject you think
about. Color as much of your brain as you believe you might use
each day for that subject. (Remember: the things you think about
the most should take up the most space in your brain picture.)

family (red)   toys & play (orange)
pets (blue)   school (yellow)
food (green)   friends (purple)
watching TV (brown)   helping others (black)

_____   _____

Use the blanks to add some ideas of your own.

FIND +
COLOR

My Name Is _____

Stars in Your Eyes

Follow the dotted lines to cut out the eyes of this funny mask.
Then color and cut out the mask and the starry wheels on the next page.
Use brads to attach the wheels to the back of the mask, matching the x's.
Turn the wheels to make your masked creature see stars that go together.

Note: When you are finished with the matching game, detach the
wheels and wear the mask just for fun!

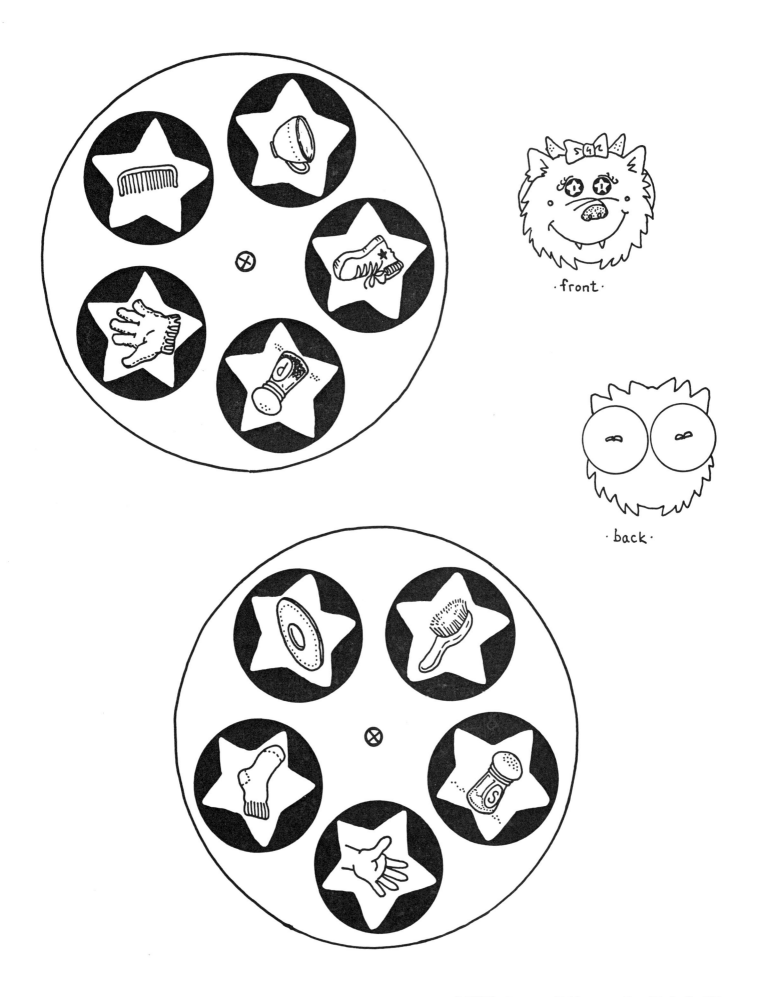

front

back

Shape Shop

If you have scissors, paste, crayons, and the shapes on this page,
what can you make?
Cut carefully on the heavy outside lines.
Assemble the pieces in your own special way.
Surprise yourself and friends!

What can you make with these shapes?

Adopt a Lemon!

Or . . . you may adopt a potato or a squash or a prune, or any fruit
or vegetable you wish.
Then sit down and get acquainted with your new friend!

Ask yourself these questions about your fruit or vegetable.
Ask someone to help you record your answers.

How does it look?

What shape is it?

What color is it?

Does it have any peculiar humps or lumps?

Does it have any interesting marks?

Is it pretty or ugly?

What word describes its looks perfectly?

How would you describe its size?

How does it feel?

Think of some words that tell how it feels to touch.

Is it pleasant or unpleasant to hold?

Rub it on your cheek. How does that feel?

Is it hard or soft?

How does it smell?

Can you think of some "smell" words that describe it?

Can you think of something else that smells similar?

How does it move?

Roll your friend on the floor or on a clean table.

How does it move? Smoothly? Bumpily? In a wobbly way?

How does it sound when it moves?

How does it taste?

Wash your friend well.

Using a table knife, poke a small hole in its side.

Stick your tongue in the hole.

How would you describe the taste? Can you think of 3 words?

Now look at your word list.

WOW! What a long list!

See if you can use some of these words to introduce your fruit or vegetable to your classmates.

Watch out, Captain Crunch!

Pretend it's your job to make up a brand-new breakfast cereal for kids.
How would it look?
How would it taste?
How might it sound?
How would you get moms and dads to buy it?
What name would you give it?

Think of a name for your new cereal.
Write the name on the box below, and show how the box would look.
Then show some of the cereal in the bowl.
Write some sentences that could be used in a TV ad to sell the cereal.

My Name Is _____

Time in, Time out

Every day is made up of twenty-four hours.
Some people say time flies.
Other people say time drags.
Some people say they never have time to get everything done.
Other people say they have nothing to do all day long.
How about you?
Draw pictures on the clock face to show how you spend your time
each day.
Think carefully . . . try to show your day from the time you get up
in the morning until you go to bed at night.

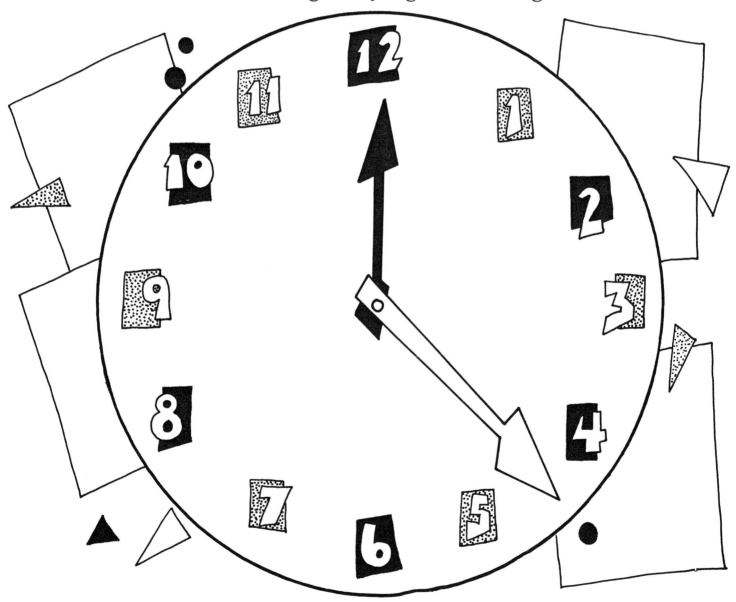

My Name Is _____

Riddle Riot

1. Using pages 29 through 34, cut on the dotted lines to make picture-window pages.
2. Fold each page in half on the solid line to make a booklet.
3. Color each figure.
4. Then close the booklet and look through the window at the colored object. (You will be able to see only part of the object.)
5. For each booklet, choose a riddle from the list below. Write the riddle that goes with each booklet on the lines under (or over) the booklet's window.
6. Use your riddle booklets to have fun with your friends.

Riddles:
      Something big is coming!
      I look scary, but I am a friend.
      No, I'm not in jail!
      Knock, knock. Is anybody home?
      Time to laugh!

What's Missing?

This is a game to play with friends or classmates or with a grownup friend.

Collect six to eight different objects from around the room.
Place them on a table.
Now turn your back and ask someone to remove one object.
Turn around and see if you can name the object that has been removed.
Do it again and see if you can name the second item that is missing.
Continue until all the objects have been taken away.

When you get good at this game, you may increase the number of objects,
OR use objects that look very much alike, such as blocks or dominoes.

Taste Testers

Choose five or six different kinds of dry cereal.
Put each kind in a bowl.
Taste one piece of each cereal by closing your eyes and letting it
melt in your mouth.
Try to remember the special taste of each one.

Then blindfold yourself.
Ask a friend to choose one piece of cereal from any bowl and place
it on your tongue.
Try to guess which cereal you are tasting.
Continue the game to see how many you can guess correctly.
Let your friends take turns too!

The Suspicion Is . . . Fishin'

If you think like a good detective, you can tell where each figure
has been and what the figures have been doing.
Look at the pictures on these two pages.
Draw lines from the figures to the places to show where each
figure has been.
Then tell what you think each figure has been doing there.
The title of this activity will give you a clue to one of the answers.

Figure

Place

Place

Place

Figure

Figure

WELCOME TO
JEFFERSON SCHO[OL]

CIRCUS

Place

Figure

Place

Figure

My Name Is _____

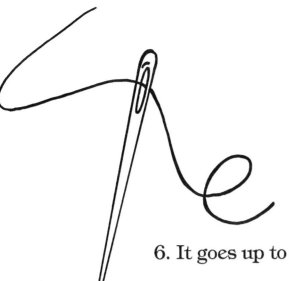

5. It's full of holes, but still holds water.

6. It goes up to the house, but never goes in.

7. It has an eye, but can't see.

8. It waves, but has no hands.

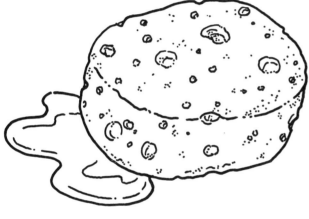

My Name Is _____

Think Five

Use your best creative thinking skills to complete the chart.
Try to list five items in each category.
Each word must begin with the letter you see in the box at the left.

Animals	People	Foods
T	T	T ....
H	H	H ....
I	I	I ....
N	N	N ....
K	K	K ....

My Name Is _____

Mitten Match

On the first snowy day of the season, these kittens want to go out
to play. Mother says:

"Last night you lost your mittens,
You naughty kittens,
When you went out to play.
Before you go to play today,
Your mittens you must find."

Look carefully at the kittens' jackets and hats.
Then look at all the mittens.
Decide which mittens belong to which kittens.
Draw a line from each set of mittens to its owner.

My Name Is _____

ABC Veggies

Pretend that you are visiting a large grocery store where you see all the beautiful vegetables arranged in the bins of the produce section.
Or think about walking through a farmer's garden in summer.
Or picture all the wonderful choices you see behind the glass in a large cafeteria restaurant or salad bar.

See if you can think of the name of a delicious vegetable for each letter of the alphabet.
Write each vegetable's name by the right letter of the alphabet.
Then see if you can draw a picture of the vegetable.
Perhaps you can think of MORE than one vegetable for each ABC letter!

A _____

B _____

C _____

D _____

E _____

F _____

G _____
H _____
I _____
J _____
K _____
L _____
M _____
N _____
O _____
P _____

Q _____
R _____
S _____
T _____
U _____
V _____
W _____
X _____
Y _____
Z _____

BEST SEEDS TURNIP

NEW KOHLRABI NK

75 BEST SEEDS ENDIVE

PARSNIPS

My Name Is _____

Pollution Solution

Look at the beginning thoughts below and draw a picture to finish each thought.

Something that people do to pollute the air we breathe is

Let's do our part!

Something that boys and girls can do to help prevent pollution is

Some things that can be recycled for reuse are

One way that boys and girls can encourage adults to reuse and recycle the earth's resources is

Let's do our part!

My Name Is _____

Snatcher's Nightmare

A thief, or a snatcher, doesn't like to be laughed at. He likes to think
he is making people mad or sad. But you can outsmart the snatcher!
Pretend a snatcher has stolen all the crayons, pens, pencils, markers,
typewriters, and computers in your town. Outsmart him by thinking of
at least ten other things you could write with.
Laugh at the snatcher! Look what we can use to write . . .

1. _____

2. _____

3. _____

4. _____

5. _____

6. _____

7. _____

8. _____

9. _____

10. _____

My Name Is _____

Who Could It Be?

Next to each group of objects, draw a picture to show who may own the objects.

POOCHIE

BUILD

BUILD-IT

My Name Is _____

Save the Turtle!

Turtle is hot and very thirsty.
He needs to get to the pond as quickly as possible.
Draw a line that will show him how to find the shortest way
to the pond.

My Name Is _____

Com"pair"ing

Look carefully at the pairs of pictures on this page.
Tell what is the same about the objects in each pair.
Then tell what is different.

Can you tell how a cat and lion are like an airplane and bird?
That's a hard one—but you can do it!

What's Wrong?
What's Right?

Add at least five things to each picture that would normally
be found in that place.

Then add five things that don't belong.

See if your friends or classmates can correctly identify
each group of pictures

You may use the pictures at the bottom of each page,
or you may draw your own pictures.

My Name Is _____

57

There's a Monkey among Us!

This is a game that is fun to play with friends and classmates.
Each person needs to identify one or two true things about him- or
herself that no one else in the group is likely to know.

For instance, what if someone in your group owns a monkey, but
the rest of you don't know it?
Perhaps someone has a mole on his big toe.
Someone else may have an aunt named Matilda.

Write your secret on the "secret fact" page.
Don't tell anyone what you write.
Then display all the pages on a wall or bulletin board.
Under each page, attach an envelope in which people can put their
"guesses" about whose secret is on that page.
After a few days, open the envelopes and see how many facts are
still secret!

SHHH! IT'S A SECRET !!

Diamond, Diamond— Who Gets the Diamond?

Pretend you are in a restaurant, eating a big bowl of spaghetti.
Suddenly you bite into something hard.
You spit it out in your hand.
It's a real diamond, and it is worth a lot of money.
No one knows where the diamond came from or how it got into the spaghetti.

Who should get to keep the diamond?

You?
The restaurant owner?
The waiter who brought you the spaghetti?
The cook who made the spaghetti?
The farmer who grew the tomatoes?
The landlord who owns the restaurant building?
The person who pays for the meal?

Write your opinion in the space below.

My Opinion

I think _____

should keep the diamond because _____

_____

_____

_____

My Name Is _____

Who's Been Sitting in My Chair?

Pretend that you have left the room for a short time.
When you return, you find this note on your chair.
Read the note to see if you can guess who came to visit
while you were gone.

I came to look for nuts, but I couldn't find any. I got a little dirt on your chair, so I dusted it with my bushy tail. I must hurry home to make a nest and fill my cupboard for winter. Sorry I missed you!

Then cut out the notes on the next two pages and
leave them on the chairs of several friends or classmates.
See if they can guess who wrote each note.
Use the blank note to write a message
from a secret guest of your choice.

61

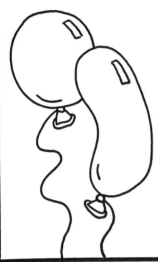

Have you seen my nose?
I seem to have lost it. Perhaps I
mixed it up with my polka dots or my
juggling balls.   Whoops! Gotta go!
I hear the ringmaster's whistle!

I AM GETTING VERY TIRED
OF SITTING ON AN EGG THAT I
AM TRYING TO HATCH FOR A
FRIEND, SO I AM SENDING A
MESSENGER TO SEE IF YOU CAN
HELP ME OUT. HAVE YOU EVER
HATCHED AN EGG?
IT TAKES LOTS
OF PATIENCE!

SAVE THE RAINFORESTS
PLEASE!

I tried your chair.
It is just my size.
I once visited a
family where one chair
was too big, one chair was
too small, and another chair
broke when I sat in it!
Yours is just right!

CUT

Your chair is quite small, but I rested awhile. Since I married a prince, I am used to sitting on a big velvet chair in a palace.

P.S. I seem to have lost my glass slipper again! Have you found it? I can't keep track of it!

My favorite thing to do is to climb up on someone's chair to frighten them. But you surprised me by not being there. You didn't even leave any curds and whey!

ARACHNID CLUB
☆ CHARTER MEMBER ☆

SMILE.
HAVE A NICE DAY

Math Smart

Collect ten buttons, pebbles, or bottlecaps.
Place the ten objects in a straight line in front of you.
Arrange and rearrange the ten objects to make as many math
problems as you can.

Here are three to get you started.

$4 + 6 = 10$

$10 - 3 = 7$

$5 + 5 = 10$

My Name Is _____

Riddle Match-up

Read the silly riddles carefully.
Then select the picture that best answers each riddle.
Draw a line to match each riddle with the correct picture box.
After all the riddles and picture boxes are matched, draw a line
from each word or phrase to name each picture box.

1. What do hippopotamuses have that no other animal has?
2. What would you have if you crossed a butterfly and a bumblebee?
3. Where does December come before July?
4. What gets bigger the more you take away from it?

dictionary   butter bee

baby hippopotamuses   hole

My Name Is _____

A Funny Garden

What a funny garden!
After last night's storm, everything here is topsy-turvy.
Help "fix-up this mix-up" by finding and circling
twelve things that are out of place.
Look closely—some are hard to find.

My Name Is _____

School Days, School Days, Dear Old Golden Rule Days

Sometimes kids wonder why grownups make the rules they do.
In the boxes below, you have a chance to express your feelings
about some rules you are expected to obey.

A school rule that I think is unfair is...

A rule I would change if I were teacher for a day is...

A rule that I think would make our school a nicer place is...

A school rule that I really like is...

My Name Is _____

Bodies, Boots, and Jelly Beans

Suppose you did not have any real measuring tools.
Could you still find out how long or how wide or how far around
something is?

Think of three unusual things with which you could measure
length or distance.
For instance, you could measure the width of a room, using just
bodies.
Ask your friends or classmates to help you experiment.
Lie down on the floor, placing your bodies head-to-toe in a straight
line across the room.
See how many bodies wide the room is!

Can you use boots or shoes to measure the length of a table?

See if you can measure the distance
around a plate by using beads or
jelly beans.

How many more unusual
tools can you use to
measure?

THINK!

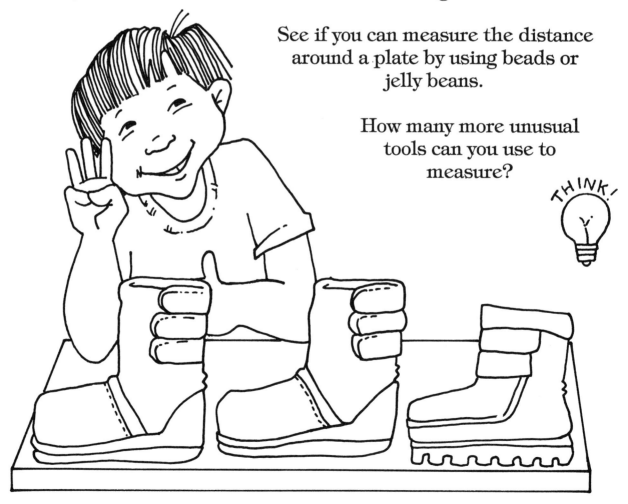

Label Able

Help Mr. Goody the grocer get his new shop ready for opening day.
Cut out the labels at the bottom of the page.
Paste each one on the correct shelf.

ONIONS

PEPPERS

APPLES

POTATOES

CANNED FRUIT

CANNED VEGETABLES

What Has Happened?

Read each sentence and look closely at the picture.
Then draw your answer to the question in the circle.

1. The flowers are broken and wilted.
   What do you think has happened?

2. The child is crying.
   What do you think has happened?

3. The boys are dripping wet.
   How do you think they got so wet?

4. The kitten is scared.
   What do you think frightened it?

70

5. The children are laughing.
   What has made them laugh?

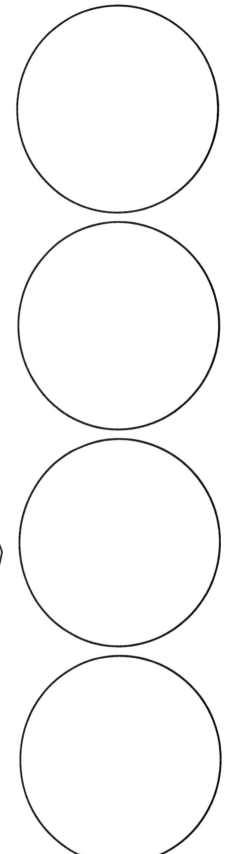

6. The man is running.
   What has happened to make him
   go so fast?

7. The house is on fire.
   What has happened to make it burn?

8. The girl is holding her tummy.
   What do you think happened to
   make her feel sick?

My Name Is _____

People Are Important

Think about the people around you and how each plays an important part in your life.
Finish the sentence OR draw a picture in each frame below to show a friend, a family member, a teacher, a neighbor, or someone else who is important to you.

I like to play with...

I would like to go to the zoo with...

I would like to take a trip with ...

I really like to be with...

My Name Is _____

Birds of a Feather

Can you tell what the items in each of these groups of four
have in common with the other items in the group?
Whisper your answers to a friend or classmate.
See if your friend agrees with you.

Group 1
robin
sparrow
crow
duck

Group 6
hands
face
hours
minutes

Group 2
Susie
Judy
Elizabeth
Mary

Group 7
Daisy
Mum
Petunia
Rose

Group 3
plane
train
boa
bike

Group 8
ruler
thermometer
scales
tablespoon

Group 4
igloo
tepee
apartment
nest

Group 9
book
letter
magazine
stop sign

Group 5
tongue
toe
knuckle
knee

Group 10
cup
pig
dog
leg

Learning about You

One of the ways someone can learn about how people live in other countries is by looking at the things these other people use every day.

Pretend that you have been asked to collect items to help children in a faraway land understand your life at home and at school.

Draw pictures in the box below to show the items you would send to the faraway children.

My Name Is _____

Teacher Notes

Rock and Roll

Ask the students to participate in creating a collection of small- to medium-sized stones and rocks. Use the collection to practice classification skills by dividing the rocks into groups, using texture, shape, size, and "roll-ability" as criteria for inclusion in a group. Ask students to record their findings by marking columns on the board or on a chart.

Inventors at Work

Create a collection of household items. Spread them on a table. Ask students to think about the useful objects that could be created by using a combination of at least three of the items. See how many different combinations they can assemble and ask them to explain the function of each combination.

Makin' Music

Assemble as many of the following as possible: bottles, boxes, plastic bowls, cups and containers, cans, sticks and stones, beans or pebbles, toothpicks, carpenter's nails, table knives, and spoons. Ask students to imagine how these items could be used to create a variety of musical instruments. Allow them to experiment in order to see how many different kinds of rhythm instruments they might invent. Let each take a turn demonstrating the sounds his or her instrument can make.

Volume Shareholders

Find five or six containers of different shapes but of similar sizes. Tell students that it is their responsibility to figure out which will hold the greatest volume of liquid or dry material. They may "guesstimate" first, then conduct experiments to determine an accurate answer.

Where Did I Come from?

Use the five-minute breaks or transition moments just before or after lunch or recess to present an object to the class. Ask the students to think about the object's origin. Where did it come from? How was it made? How did it get from raw materials to its present form? This activity demands some good thinking skills and promises fascinating discussion! Suggested objects: a shoe, a flower, gelatin, a light bulb, bubblegum, a book, a silk scarf, a fork, a tea bag.

> *P.S. You may have to do a little research in order to lead the discussion.*
> *There's no need to let the discussion get too complicated or too deep.*
> *Accept all ideas and ask the students to decide if the ideas are plausible.*

Food for Thought

Collect a stack of discarded frozen-meal boxes that display pictures of the meals. Give each student a box and ask him or her to think about where the items in that meal originated and how they were prepared for packaging. This is a wonderful exercise in sequential and critical thinking.

Connect the Clues

Divide students into small groups and give each group a set of simple clues. Ask group members to think about how the clues could be connected as bits of evidence that will construct a story that might explain a "crime."

Example:
1. All the potted flowers are turned over on a porch.
2. There is fur caught on the edge of a screen door.
3. The cat's dish is missing.
4. Someone heard strange noises in the night.

Example:
1. A clown suddenly shows up in a kindergarten room.
2. The kindergarten teacher is missing.
3. A fake moustache is found in the school restroom.
4. A kindergarten student is wearing very heavy lipstick.

Prediction

Play games with the child such as "What would happen if . . ." in order to encourage predicting skills.

A Walking Tour

Take a walking tour of the neighborhood. Carry a magnifying glass and help the child look for things he or she would never have noticed before.

Questions of the Encouraging Kind

Ask open-ended questions which encourage thoughtful answers and follow-up discussions.

Stretching Thinking Skills

Play games in which the child must follow directions. Gradually make the directions more complex in order to stretch thinking skills.

Story Starters

Provide a beginning or end of a story (or both) and ask the child to finish it.

Making Use of Color

Provide for creative art experiences using finger paints, chalk, and paper. Ask the child to select colors to represent different emotions. Examples: fear, anger, happiness, sadness, excitement.

Cooking and Science

Plan simple cooking and science experiments that include egg-preparing processes such as frying, boiling, scrambling, beating, and whipping in order to discover how air, heat, and water affect the consistency of eggs.

About the Environment

Fly a kite, sail a toy boat in a stream, use a strainer to explore a puddle, or blow dandelions or milkweed seed pods in the wind to help the child develop environmental awareness and curiosity.

Personality Puzzles

Use a slide projector or a directional lamp and heavy tagboard to make a silhouette head of each student. Ask each student to write on his or her own silhouette some words that describe the kind of person he or she is. (Write common words on the board to help with writing and spelling.) A student may trade silhouettes with a friend and ask the friend to add some words. Encourage students to write their words in large print and in random order with plenty of space between words.

When word collections are complete, use the silhouettes in one of the following ways:

1. Allow students to draw one silhouette from a stack of silhouettes and introduce the person whose silhouette was drawn, using some of the words written on the silhouette. The class must guess which student is being described.
2. Allow each student to carefully cut his or her figure into five or six pieces, creating a puzzle that may be kept in an envelope to reassemble for fun at a later time.

Riddle Secrets

Spread a random collection of 12 to 14 objects on a table. Ask students to secretly choose one of the objects and make up a riddle about it. Plan a time when students can try guessing the answers to their classmates' riddles, guessing which object is the answer to each.

A Is for Action

Assign each student a letter of the alphabet. Ask the student to make a list of as many action words as possible that begin with that letter. Cover a chalkboard or chart with all the words generated by the students. Then ask each student to compose an action story, using the list as a resource.

Object-tivity

Give each student an object. Ask the student to observe all the physical qualities of the object. Ask each to think of at least ten words that could be associated with the object. Place students in groups of three or four, and ask them to share the words they have chosen. Other members of the small group may contribute to the other students' word lists.

How Do You Do?

Write the following questions on a chart and go over them together.

1. Where were you born?
2. When is your birthday?
3. What are your favorite foods? Colors? Toys? Books?
4. If you could go anywhere in the world, what place would you choose?
5. If you could have one special wish, what would you ask for?
6. What interesting job would you like to have when you grow up?

Explain to the students that these are the kinds of questions used to interview a person about his or her life. Choose a literary character. Ask students to pretend they have interviewed the character, using some or all of the above questions. What answers did they get?

Recycle the Comics

Recycle the comics to encourage creative thinking and composing!

1. Cut Sunday comic strips into single-frame sections and place in envelopes, one envelope for each strip. Ask the child to arrange the sections from one envelope in the proper sequence. Then ask the child to create his or her own version of the events in the strip.
2. Cut apart and arrange all the sections of a comic strip in order, leaving out the last section. Read and enjoy each section with the child, then ask the child to develop an "ending" for the story.

3. Remove all the "talk balloons" from a simple comic strip. Ask the child to make up the conversation that might be taking place in each section.
4. Help the child arrange the events of a simple nursery rhyme such as "Little Jack Horner," "Humpty Dumpty," or "Little Miss Muffet" to form a comic strip. Supply paper and crayons and encourage the child to draw his or her own interpretation of the rhyme in comic strip fashion, but supplying different characters, a different sequence of events, or a surprise ending. Write the "talk" in the talk balloons as dictated by the child.

Encouraging Creative and Critical Thinking

Ask the child questions such as these:
1. Can you name two animals and four insects that have wings?
2. Can you tell the names of ten fruits that grow on trees?
3. Can you name two things with two wheels, three things with three wheels, and four things with four wheels?
4. Can you name one person who is one year younger than you are, two people who are two years older than you are, and three people who are three years older?

Be sure to allow plenty of time to discuss the answers . . . and to encourage the child to think of questions to ask you!

What Would You Do If . . . ?

You can provoke open-ended and imaginative "brain straining" with the use of "What would you do if . . . ?" questions like these.
1. What would you do if you opened the front door to see a spaceship landing in your front yard?
2. What would you do if you awakened in the middle of the night to see circus clowns, elephants, kangaroos, and a marching band parading down your street?
3. What would you do if you could take a trip anywhere in the world you wanted to go?
4. What would you do if you could give any present of your choice to one person in the world?

Stimulate Higher-level Thinking

The activities and projects in this book were developed to encourage young children to open their minds, stretch their imaginations, and "think through" the many wonders of their daily lives. The puzzles, games, songs, poems, art, drama, music, literature, writing, science, math, and social studies projects can help the child use new and different methods to solve problems, to observe people, place, and things in a new light, and to grow in "brain power."

The reference guide based on Bloom's Taxonomy on page 79 will be helpful when planning additional experiences to encourage the child to develop and use higher-order thinking skills.

Quick Reference Guide Based on Bloom's Taxonomy for Incorporating Thinking Skills into Activities for Young Children

Stages	Selected Trigger Verbs		Selected Activities
Knowledge			
recalling, restating, and remembering learned information	choose recall match read	find identify list write	recite nursery rhymes, ABCs, numbers; label leaves, pictures; copy images; sing songs, play games
Comprehension			
grasping meaning of information by interpreting and translating what has been learned	associate change define recognize	summarize estimate contrast explain	draw, paint, sculpt; group objects; find hidden pictures; sequence events
Application			
making use of information in context different from the one in which it was learned	apply choose classify produce	modify predict record experiment	classify objects, ideas, words; make up new endings; conduct science experiments; construct models
Analysis			
breaking learned information into its component parts	analyze discover sort survey	divide infer simplify compare	question; solve problems; tell "what if"; compare and contrast objects, ideas; discuss
Synthesis			
creating new information and ideas using what has been learned previously	blend build combine compose	rearrange design devise imagine	make collages; create original stories, poems; create/modify games, skits, puppet shows; design word problems
Evaluation			
making judgments about learned information on the basis of established criteria	assess judge measure test	determine rate rank justify	design and present awards; make up and take quizzes; have discussions and debates; make up rating scales